Contents

Happy Campers in the Sun

The children have had a fabulous camping trip. The sun has shone nearly every day so they've had loads of fun. It's been warm enough to swim in the lake and paddle in the river.

The nights have been hot so they've been able to stay up late. They've sung, danced and cooked marshmallows around the campfire. Everyone agrees it is the hottest summer they can remember.

WILD WEATHER

Written by
Liz Gogerly

Illustrated by
Sr. Sánchez

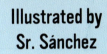

W
FRANKLIN WATTS

Franklin Watts

First published in Great Britain in 2020
by The Watts Publishing Group
© The Watts Publishing Group 2020

Managing editor: Victoria Brooker
Design: Little Red Ant

ISBN: 978 1 4451 6854 8 (hbk)
ISBN: 978 1 4451 6855 5 (pbk)

Printed in China

Franklin Watts
An imprint of Hachette Children's Group
Part of The Watts Publishing Group
Carmelite House
50 Victoria Embankment
London EC4Y 0DZ
An Hachette UK Company

www.hachette.co.uk
www.franklinwatts.co.uk

MIX
Paper from
responsible sources
FSC® C104740

WILD WEATHER FACTS

In recent years many parts of the world have experienced long spells of hot weather during the summer. We call these periods of high temperatures 'heat waves'. Scientists believe that we will experience more heat waves due to climate change and global warming.

Look at poor Basil – he's a real hot dog!

TAKE ACTION!

It's important that we all stay safe in the sun. Everyone should protect themselves by covering up and using sun protection. On very hot days, drinking cool drinks and seeking the shade are a must, too.

Extreme heat is particularly dangerous for the very young and old or people that are already ill. Heat stroke is a serious condition which occurs when a person's temperature goes above 103°F (39.4°C) – this can lead to heart attacks and breathing problems.

It's Raining, it's Pouring

Everything changes in the middle of the night. At first the children hear the patter of light rain on their tent. Quickly, the rain gets heavier and lashes down so hard they think the tent might leak. Finally, there are massive crashes of thunder and lightning – it really is frightening.

In the morning, the children look out of their tent at the dark grey skies as droplets of rain are still falling. The campsite is soaking wet. Nobody forecast this – or did they?

MAKE A REMARKABLE RAIN GAUGE

Measure the amount of rain that falls in your area using your own homemade rain gauge.

Scissors, ruler or a bendy tape measure

What you need:

Reuse an empty 2-litre plastic drink bottle

Paper, waterproof pen and some masking tape

Instructions:

1) Remove the labels from the bottle and give it a clean. Cut around the bottle just below the neck. You will need sharp scissors for this task so you might need to ask an adult for help.

2) The top part of the bottle will act as a funnel and will stop water from evaporating. Turn it upside down and slide it into the bottom section of the bottle.

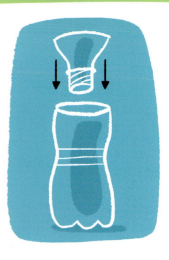

3) Stick some masking tape vertically on the bottle. Use the bendy tape measure or ruler and the pen to mark off a scale in cm.

4) Find a place outside in the open so the rain gauge can collect all the rain that falls. To stop it blowing over, dig a hole in the ground and bury the gauge so that just 5 cm pokes out.

5) Check your rain gauge at the same time every day. Measure the rain and keep a record in a weather diary.

6) After each measurement, empty the gauge ready for the next day.

Wonderful Weather

It is miserable packing up to go home. Everything is soaking wet. But everyone agrees it has been a brilliant holiday. As they pack and fold everything away the children think about the weather they love the most.

▲ Mason raves about the snow. It's such fun to go sledging and snowballing. He loves making snow dogs most of all ...

◄ Lulu loves it when the wind blows around the colourful autumn leaves. The trees look so beautiful.

Noah actually likes the rain, but he prefers it when he's tucked up in bed at home or watching a film on the sofa where he feels cosy and safe. ▶

▶ Anjali is thrilled by thunder and lightning. She counts the seconds between the flash of lightning and rumble of thunder.

WILD WEATHER FACTS

Big raindrops fall quicker than smaller drops. A large drop may fall at a speed of 32 km/h (20 mph) – the speed limit for cars in some city centres!

NOW YOU TRY ...

Thunder is heard after the lightning strike because the speed of light is faster than the speed of sound. So when you count the seconds between the flash and clap of thunder you can find out how far away the storm is approximately.

5 seconds = 1 mile = 1.6 km; 10 seconds = 2 miles = 3.2 km; 15 seconds = 3 miles = 4.8 km

Kicking up a Storm

The children spend the journey home sharing facts about different types of wild weather. They know that some weather can be extremely dangerous.

Like hurricanes ...

Lulu can't believe that these powerful storms can have winds of up to 251 km/h (156 mph). No wonder they cause so much damage!

And tornadoes ...

Noah says that these swirling winds can travel between 16-32 km/h (10-20 mph). They mostly happen in the USA where they cause havoc when they strike.

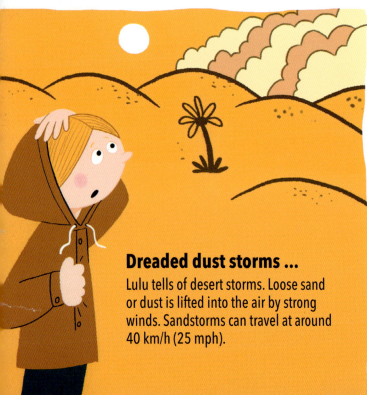

Dreaded dust storms ...

Lulu tells of desert storms. Loose sand or dust is lifted into the air by strong winds. Sandstorms can travel at around 40 km/h (25 mph).

And bitter blizzards

When snow in the sky and snow on the floor are whipped up by strong winds of over 56 km/h (35 mph) we experience blizzards. Mason nearly got lost in one last year ...

MAKE A TORNADO IN A JAR

Whip up a storm in your kitchen and create your own tornado in a jar. In fact you are creating a water vortex, but this is the nearest you'll get to a tornado (we hope).

Food colouring or glitter

Water

What you need:

A glass jar with a screw-on lid

Washing-up liquid or liquid handwash

Instructions:

2) Squeeze in a few squirts of washing-up liquid.

1) Fill the jar with water nearly to the top.

3) Add a few drops of food colouring and/or glitter and put the lid on.

4) Turn the jar upside down and grip it with both hands. Quickly spin the jar in a circular motion.

5) Watch carefully as a water vortex forms.

11

The Magical Fire Rainbow

After the summer holidays the children go back to school. The sun is shining as they walk up to the school gate. But just then it begins to rain too. Noah gets really excited when he spots a rainbow. The weather can be so magical.

GET BUSY

You can make a rainbow with a torch, a sheet of white paper and a glass of water. Simply place the glass on the paper and move the torch around until the rainbow appears on the paper. You could try the same experiment without a torch on a sunny day using the light of the sun instead.

Mr Sangar is waiting to hear about the children's holidays.
He is pleased to hear the children are so enthusiastic about the
weather because they are going to learn more about it this year.

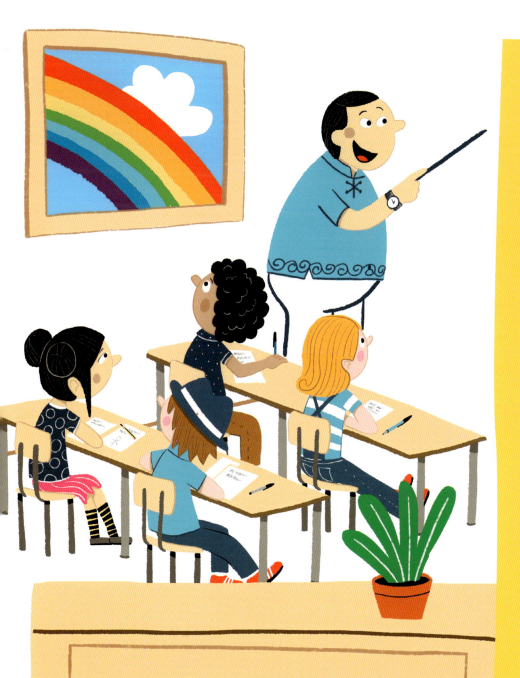

Noah tells Mr Sangar about the
rainbow and so Mr Sangar tells the
class about a 'fire rainbow' – a very
rare and wonderful thing ...

WILD WEATHER FACTS

WHAT'S A RAINBOW?
A rainbow is a multi-coloured arc
that appears in the sky. It usually
happens when the sun is shining
and it's raining at the same time.

HOW IS IT FORMED?
Sunlight appears white but it's
really a spectrum of colours: red,
orange, yellow, green, blue, indigo
and violet. When sunlight passes
through raindrops the light is
dispersed into the different colours .

WHAT IS AN
UPSIDE-DOWN RAINBOW?
It's like a smile in the sky. It is
much rarer than a rainbow and it
only happens when sunlight shines
through ice crystals high in
the sky.

WHAT IS A FIRE RAINBOW?
This extraordinary display happens
when light from the Sun or Moon
passes through ice crystals high up
in the sky, more often in wispy
cirrus clouds.

CAN YOU HAVE A
RAINBOW AT NIGHT?
A moonbow happens when the
Moon is bright and it's raining.

Blown Away by Weather

Weather is part of our everyday lives but what is it? Mr Sangar explains that weather is about what's happening in the atmosphere. There are six major things going on up there that are constantly changing and making our weather.

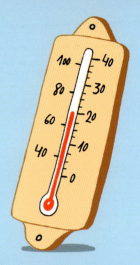

GUIDE TO THE BIG SIX

2 Temperature

The measure of how hot or cold the atmosphere is. We use a thermometer to measure in Celsius (°C) or Fahrenheit (°F).

1 Atmospheric pressure

The weight of the atmosphere that surrounds the Earth. The weight of the air can be measured with a barometer. Air pressure falls as the weight of air decreases. In weather, there are low and high pressure systems.

3 Precipitation

All kinds of water that form in the atmosphere and fall from the sky. Precipitation includes rain, snow, sleet, frost, hail and even dew.

4 Wind

Wind is the movement of air caused by the differences in temperature and atmospheric pressure on the Earth. Wind direction and the speed of wind help to make our weather.

GET BUSY

Next time you go for a walk look up and look out for weather vanes – you'll often see them at the highest point of a building. These instruments have a pointer (arrow) which moves and points towards the direction the wind is coming from. When the arrow points to the east then the wind is coming from the east.

5 Humidity

This is how much water vapour is in the atmosphere or air. Cold air holds less water than warm air. This affects how hot we feel; for example on a hot and humid day you'll probably feel sticky and uncomfortable. On a sunny day that is less humid you will feel cooler.

6 Cloud cover

Clouds have cooling and warming effects on the weather. Rather like a blanket they can keep the heat of the sun in. However, sometimes they move over the sun and block the heat. When there are no clouds then all of the sun's heat reaches the Earth's surface.

Understanding the Water Cycle

One weekend the children pile off to the countryside. Unfortunately, it doesn't stop raining. Out come the umbrellas and welly boots. So, where does rain come from? Mason's dad talks to them about the amazing journey that water makes. "Water never leaves the planet," he explains. "It goes round and round in a process we call the water cycle." He explains about the different stages.

Groundwater

1. Evaporation

The sun heats up the Earth and the water in the oceans, rivers, streams and lakes. As the temperature of the water rises, some of the water evaporates and turns into a gas called vapour.

16

Sun

Precipitation – rain, snow, sleet, hail etc.

Hills

Vapour

River

Ocean

3. Precipitation

The clouds gradually get heavier with moisture. Eventually it falls to Earth as rain, snow, sleet or hail.

2. Condensation

The water vapour is light and rises into the air and begins to cool down. As the vapour cools, it turns into water droplets and forms clouds. High in the sky the clouds move around.

4. Collection

Precipitation falls into the rivers, lakes and oceans as well as on the land. Some water is used by us or by plants and animals. Other water evaporates and the water cycle starts all over again.

Rain, Snow, Sleet or Hail?

Over the next few months the children experience precipitation in all its shapes and sizes. Lulu discovers that she doesn't mind sloshing through the rain any more. It is amazing to think that those raindrops are falling from clouds situated about 8 to 16 km (4–11 miles) above her head. And that sometimes you can smell the rain before it falls. This scent is called 'petrichor' and it's Lulu's favourite smell.

WILD WEATHER FACTS

The highest amount of rainfall recorded in one day was at Foc-Foc in La Réunion in January 1966. In 24 hours, 182.37 cm of rain fell.

And who knew that raindrops are not really that classic tear shape. They come in all shapes and sizes and change as they fall to the ground.

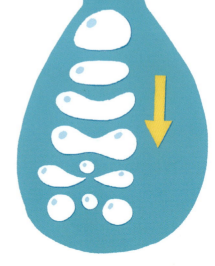

Meanwhile, Mason's found out that snowflakes are not just frozen raindrops, they are made from snow crystals. These form when water vapour in the clouds freezes.

Every snow crystal is different but each one starts as a small hexagonal shape. As the crystal falls through the sky it grows and changes shape in a unique way.

WILD WEATHER FACTS

The biggest hailstone ever recorded is believed to have fallen in Cordoba, Argentina in February 2018. It measured a whopping 23 cm, which is bigger than your average football!

Anjali thinks there's nothing more disappointing than sleet. It's made from a mixture of snow and rain and it is no good for making snowballs or snow dogs!

Noah has never forgotten the day he played football and it hailed. Hailstones are frozen water formed high up in thunderstorm clouds. Noah says they felt like icy bullets.

Ouch!

Head in the Clouds

Every autumn Mason stays at Uncle Mac's farm. His uncle doesn't watch weather forecasts. He looks up at the clouds and they tell him what he needs to know about the weather.

Cumulus

On a fair and sunny day those great puffy clouds that you see are likely to be cumulus. As heated air rises from the ground it cools and the water vapour condenses to create these fluffy, cotton-wool clouds.

Cirrus

Wispy and wavy, these clouds appear all year round. They're whiter than other clouds because of the ice crystals which they're made from. Cirrus clouds are a sign of change – often warmer weather is on the way!

Altocumulus

These clumps of fluffy clouds are a sign of settled weather. They're made up of ice and water but they rarely mean it'll rain.

Stratus

On dull grey days, you're probably looking up at stratus clouds. Even though they may be quite dark and thick there is little chance of heavy rainfall.

WILD WEATHER FACTS

The clouds in the sky are actually very heavy. Those fluffy cumulus clouds way up high may look light but they're huge and filled with water droplets. The average cumulus cloud weighs in at around 500,000 kg.

That's the same as:

3 whales

OR

38 buses

Stratocumulus

These are the most common type of cloud in the sky. They are actually stratus clouds breaking up and they are around in all kinds of weather – dry or wet.

GET BUSY

Go cloudspotting! Look out for cumulus clouds as they begin to grow upwards and predict whether rain is on its way. See if you can spot 'mackerel skies' and keep track on whether or not the weather does change.

Cumulonimbus

Watch out if those cumulus clouds keep on growing. Soon they may be great towers of billowing clouds called cumulonimbus. They bring rain showers or even thunderstorms.

Cirrocumulus

A large patch of these small white clouds look like fish's scales, which is why we call them 'mackerel skies'. These clouds don't bring rain but they often mean it's on its way. Enjoy the sun while it lasts!

Altostratus

These large sheets of thin cloud allow a little sunlight to shine through. They're not particularly interesting to look at but they do suggest that a change of weather is on the way.

Nimbostratus

When you look up and see continuous dark grey clouds above then the chances are you're looking at nimbostratus. These clouds block out the sun and bring rain or even snow. If you see these clouds you know it may rain for a few hours!

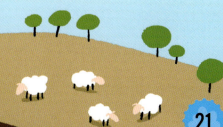

Meet the Experts!

Nobody knows more about the weather than a meteorologist, someone who is qualified to study the weather. Mr Sangar takes the class on a trip to the 'Met Office' where a whole team of meteorologists work together to predict the weather.

By using a mixture of science, maths and data collected from weather stations and weather satellites they can produce the weather forecast. They can make long-term predictions about our weather, such as upcoming storms or extreme heat.

WILD WEATHER FACTS

Weather affects everything we do so it's no wonder we have so many weather stations and other forms of data collection going on around the world.

Around the world, there are 10,000 land weather stations, 1,000 upper-air weather stations, 7,000 weather stations on ships, 100 moored stations and 1,000 drifting buoys that record the weather. There are also about 16 meteorological satellites and 50 research satellites doing the same job in space.

Weather satellites

Since the 1960s, weather satellites have been orbiting the Earth gathering information about our planet. Images of clouds, formation of storms, pollution and even volcanoes erupting are picked up by satellites. Meteorologists use all this information to track the weather.

Weather stations

Weather stations are operating all over the planet, on land and at sea, to monitor our weather. Meteorologists work at some of the stations while some stations are unmanned. Anemometers are used to measure the speed of wind, thermometers to read the temperatures and barometers to determine air pressure.

The Four Seasons

Back at school, the children learn it isn't just the atmosphere that influences the weather. The seasons help make our weather too. Most parts of the world get four seasons, but places close to the equator experience hot weather through most of the year.

Spring

Temperatures get warmer and seeds begin to grow. Spring flowers appear and buds open on the trees. Sometimes it rains and that's good because it helps everything to grow.

Summer

The hottest months of the year in many places. It's time to head outdoors and enjoy the sunshine. Crops are growing, flowers are blooming, and trees are filled with green leaves.

WILD WEATHER FACTS

The seasons in the northern and southern hemispheres are different. Australians can spend their Christmas day on the beach in scorching sunshine while in countries like the UK and USA, people huddle indoors keeping warm around a fire.

Why do we get the seasons?

The seasons happen because of the way the Earth spins on its axis as it moves around the Sun each year.

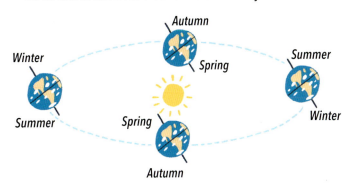

Autumn

Temperatures dip but there are still some bright, sunny days. People wrap up warmly and head out to see the leaves on the trees as they change colour. Crops are harvested.

Winter

It is usually cold in winter. Many people can't wait for a big freeze with ice and snow for playing. Some animals hibernate to escape the cold. Many trees are bare and dormant, which means they don't grow.

The Weather is Changeable

Lulu visits her grandma each winter. She packs lots of clothes because you never know what the weather will be like. This year it's icy where grandma lives. When they go for a walk Lulu pretends she's skating. Lulu asks grandma why the weather can be so changeable all the time. Grandma is no expert but these days when she listens to the weather forecast they seem to blame everything on the jet stream!

Subtropical jet stream ▼

▲ Subtropical jet stream brings hot weather

Polar front jet stream brings cold weather
▼

Lulu looks up 'jet stream' on the Internet. Jet streams are super fast winds travelling at over 320 k/ph (200 mph) high up between the troposphere and stratosphere – which is around 9–16 km (5–9 miles) up in the sky, so you can't feel these winds on the ground. They are so strong that they can steer anything from freezing cold weather to sizzling summer days our way.

GET BUSY

Learning about the weather can be fascinating. Become a weather detective and go online to discover more about: the equator, polar front jet stream, subtropical jet stream and the polar vortex.

Hurricanes Happen

One day, a massive storm lashes the coastline near the children's homes. Its powerful winds churn up the waves and blow tiles off roofs. Everyone is warned to stay indoors. This gives the children time to discover more about powerful storms.

What are hurricanes?

Enormous tropical storms form in the South Pacific and the Indian Ocean between June and the end of November each year. When a tropical storm has winds of over 119 kph (74 mph) for a set period of time, it is called a hurricane. Hurricanes are given a category from one to five – five is strongest and deadliest with the fastest winds.

What about typhoons?

These tropical storms form in the Northwest Pacific. They are the same as hurricanes but in a different place. Just like a hurricane, the clouds form a spiral and there is a spot in the middle called the eye.

The truth about twisters and tornadoes ...

These deadly storms have far greater speeds than the average hurricane. The great whirling column of air passes over land ripping up everything as it goes. The storm passes quickly – usually in less than an hour – but in that time many people can get injured or killed.

GET BUSY

During hurricane season track a hurricane and watch how it develops. Where does it land first and where does it go next? Follow its progress on weather websites. Does it cross the Atlantic and become a storm anywhere else?

I Hear Thunder

Spring brings with it sunshine and showers which also means thunderstorms and lightning. The children are at Mason's house for a sleepover when they first hear a roll of thunder.

WILD WEATHER FACTS

They say that 'lightning never strikes in the same place twice' but there is a lightning strike somewhere on the planet around 44 times every second.

Watch out: every year there are about 1.4 billion lightning strikes!

A lightning strike carries approximately 100 million volts of electricity.

Each lightning strike can be over 50,000°F – which is 5 times hotter than the Sun.

In ancient times people thought thunder was the sound of clouds crashing together. Lulu explains that thunder is the sound that is made when lightning strikes. Lightning is electricity, which is formed when frozen droplets of water bump into each other in the thunderclouds up in the sky.

What causes lightning?

In a cumulonimbus cloud, many small bits of ice bump into each other as they move around in the air. These collisions create an electric charge. After a while, the whole cloud fills up with electrical positive and negative charges. The negative charged hail collects at the bottom of the thundercloud. The positive charged ice crystals stay at the top of the thundercloud. Opposites attract so the negative charge at the bottom of the cloud seeks out a positive charge to connect with and – zap – lightning strikes. Lightning occurs inside clouds, between clouds and from clouds to the ground.

GET BUSY

See whether you can spot the different kinds of lightning next time there's a storm.

Intracloud lightning
Lightning within a cloud – sometimes called sheet lightning.

Rocket lightning
Tree-like, horizontal lightning that also happens within clouds or from cloud to ground.

Staccato
A quick flash of bright lightning.

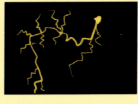

Bolt from the blue
Another form of cloud-to-ground lightning that strikes a long way from its storm cloud.

Forked lightning
Cloud-to-ground lightning that has many branches or forks.

Ribbon lightning
Wind makes this lightning strike appear like lengths of ribbon.

Bead lightning
One stage of a lightning strike that appears broken up like a string of beads.

Weather vs Climate

Noah has received a message from his brother who is on holiday in the USA. He's having fun in the sun, but why is it so hot out there? Noah's mum says it's because of the climate. Noah is confused – he thought weather and climate were the same thing.

Dear Noah

Having a great time in the hottest place on Earth. I'm in Death Valley, California, USA. It's often around 47°C (116°F) here in the summertime - imagine that! In 1913 they recorded the highest temperature ever recorded which was 56.7°C (129°F) – I'm sure you could have cooked dinner on the desert sands that day - feels like I'm cooking today!

Stay cool bro, love Josh xx

WILD WEATHER FACTS

Death Valley is so hot and dry for many reasons. Partly because it is in a long deep valley which is 86 m below sea level and also because there is little vegetation and the ground absorbs more heat and then radiates it back.

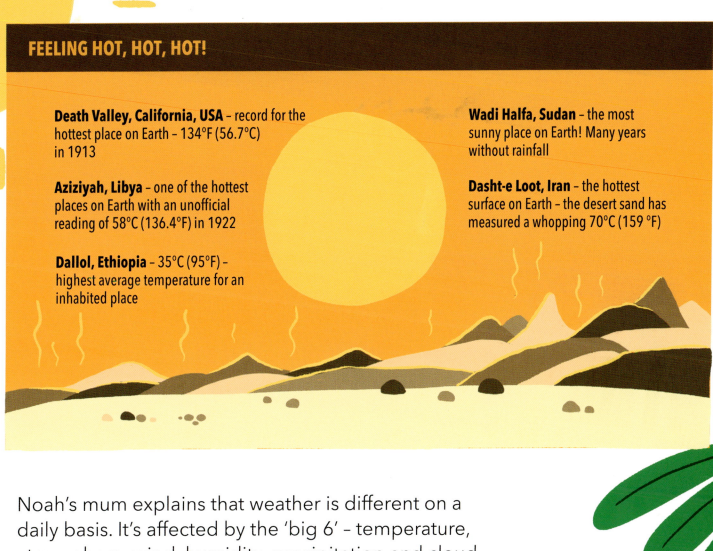

Death Valley, California, USA – record for the hottest place on Earth – 134°F (56.7°C) in 1913

Aziziyah, Libya – one of the hottest places on Earth with an unofficial reading of 58°C (136.4°F) in 1922

Dallol, Ethiopia – 35°C (95°F) – highest average temperature for an inhabited place

Wadi Halfa, Sudan – the most sunny place on Earth! Many years without rainfall

Dasht-e Loot, Iran – the hottest surface on Earth – the desert sand has measured a whopping 70°C (159 °F)

Noah's mum explains that weather is different on a daily basis. It's affected by the 'big 6' – temperature, atmosphere, wind, humidity, precipitation and cloud cover (see pages 14–15). Climate is a much bigger picture – it's the average weather that happens in a place over a longer period of time. It is influenced by many other factors, such as how far a place is from the equator, or how high up it is or how far away from the sea.

Welcome to the Climate Zones

The children start thinking about all the places they've visited in the world and the kind of climate that they've experienced ...

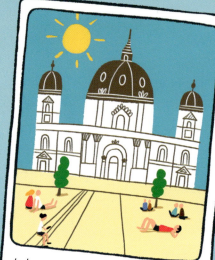

Lulu remembers the hot summer she spent in Berlin in Germany.

CONTINENTAL

In areas a long way from the sea the climate is sometimes called continental. This usually means warm or hot and humid summers with cold winters. Many places within central and northeastern parts of Europe, North America and Asia have continental climates.

Noah had a wonderful beach holiday on the Greek island of Crete.

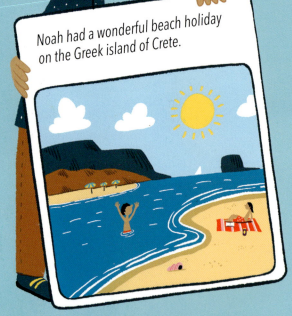

Mason reckons you can't beat camping in the countryside.

MEDITERRANEAN

Expect hot summers and cool or mild winters with moderate or lots of rainfall. Areas around the Mediterranean Sea, as well as parts of California, in the USA, South Africa; and Australia, have Mediterranean climates.

TEMPERATE

With a temperate climate the temperatures don't go up and down much and the rain is spread throughout the year. There are four definite seasons. Western Europe, parts of the west coast of North America, south-east Australia, New Zealand and South America have temperate climates.

Anjali visited her family in Sri Lanka last year – it was boiling hot!

TROPICAL

The temperatures don't vary much in these places and it's usually hot and humid with plenty of rain. These areas are located near the equator and are found in Asia, Africa and Central and South America.

Lulu's mum once visited Uluru in Australia. This famous landmark is right in the middle of an arid area.

Mason's Uncle Jack spent a year working on an oil rig in Alaska where it was dark and cold.

POLAR

Near the North or South Pole there are two seasons – summer and winter – and both are freezing cold. Alaska, in the USA, parts of Canada, Scandinavia, Iceland, and Russia have polar climates.

ARID

Arid means dry, and hot deserts are the driest and hottest places on Earth. Most deserts don't have regular seasons or rainfall. The Atacama Desert in Chile is the driest place in the world with no rainfall recorded at all at some of its weather stations. However, around Uluru, in Australia, the temperatures can range from 5°C (41°F) in July to 37°C (99°F) in January.

Clear night!

 Tropical storm

 Thunder

 Thunder shower (day)

 Thunder shower (night)

 Sunny day

 Partly cloudy (night)

 Sunny intervals

 Mist

 Fog

 Cloudy

 Overcast

Weather Watch

These days Noah has become obsessed with watching the weather forecast. Sometimes he catches it on TV. He also checks the app on his phone or the weather sites on the Internet. Now he understands all the symbols he has become quite an expert.

At the weekend, Noah enjoys looking at the weather reports from around the world. It's fascinating to see how the weather is different everywhere. At one time there may be a heat wave in Australia and snow blizzards in northern America. Or there may be heavy rains called monsoons going on in India but it's totally dry over in Indonesia.

Noah knows how to read a weather map and understands the weather fronts and the weather they may bring. Maybe one day he'll be a meteorologist!

 Light rain shower (night)

 Light rain shower (day)

 Drizzle

 Light rain

MAKE A CLOUD BURST

Get cloud bursting with this fun experiment. Imagine the shaving foam is a cloud and the food colouring is water droplets and see what happens ...

What you need:

 1 small glass

1 large glass

 Shaving cream

 Blue food colouring

 Water

Eyedropper or pipette

Light snow shower (night)

Hail

Instructions:

1) Take the small glass and add 3 tablespoons of water. Add 10 drops of food colouring to the water and mix it to make a blue liquid.

2) Fill the large glass three-quarters full of water.

3) Squirt about 6 cm of shaving foam on top of the water.

4) Use the eyedropper to add the coloured water to the shaving cream drop by drop.

5) Count the number of drops it takes before the coloured water begins to fall like rain from the shaving foam. This is when the water has become too heavy for the shaving foam to hold – just as a cloud becomes too heavy to hold moisture during the water cycle.

Before

After

Hail shower (day)

Hail shower (night)

Sleet

Sleet shower (day)

Global Warming and Freezing Winters

Sometimes when it's much colder or hotter than normal, people blame it on climate change. At school the children learn about global warming and how the temperature of the Earth is warming up and the ice at the Poles is melting. Noah is confused – why do we get icy cold winters when the world is getting hotter?

Mr Sangar explains that hot summers are contributing to the problem. Warm land temperatures affect the air high up in the atmosphere. This creates different weather patterns and can cause the jet stream to behave differently too.

Global warming is having a big effect on the cold air over the North and South Poles (polar vortices). In recent years, this cold air has got weaker and sometimes breaks up and behaves in a different way. The polar vortex over the Arctic is straying further south more often and creating the freezing winters in northern parts of the USA.

It isn't too late to reverse climate change – if we reduce the carbon emissions that contribute to global warming. Mason has joined a local conservation group that encourages people to reduce, reuse and recycle. He's also in charge of recycling at home.

PLASTIC

PAPER

Climate Change and Floods

In spring the rain doesn't stop. April showers turn to torrential rain in May. The children can't believe how high the river in town is getting. Then the river breaks its banks and their street is flooded. The fire brigade has to save people from their homes using boats.

As the world warms up, more water evaporates from the oceans and from all over the planet meaning there are more rain clouds. Warm air holds more moisture which means that when it does rain it can be heavier and cause flooding.

WILD WEATHER FACTS

In Pakistan the heaviest rainfall in 38 years was recorded in 2018. Flooding caused landslides and sinkholes, and thousands of people lost their homes to flood water. In Venice, Italy, high tides and strong winds caused 70 per cent of the city to flood. In 2019 the floods in Venice were worse, with the highest tides in fifty years. Most experts blame climate change.

GET BUSY

Across the world children are campaigning against climate change. Look up photographs taken on marches near you and see some of the placards that other children have made about climate change. Some of them are quite shocking and others are funny. Now make your own colourful sign with a catchy logo or expression about the environment.

At school, the headmistress Ms Young suggests everyone raises money to help the families affected by the floods. The children ask her why the flooding is so bad this year. Ms Young thinks that global warming is affecting the water cycle.

Surviving Snow, Storms and Heat

Weather patterns are changing. The Earth is experiencing more storms, floods and intense heat waves. People are making changes to protect themselves against extreme weather. The children discover more about what people do to protect themselves against weather around the world.

This costs more in money but saves lives.

USA
Heat waves are a killer! In the USA heat kills more people than lightning, tornadoes, hurricane or floods. Painting buildings white or using 'cooler' materials that don't absorb heat for new buildings will help in the future.

Look it actually works!

UK
Storm surges cause rivers to burst their banks and flood. Sometimes flood defence systems like walls cannot cope with water levels. In parts of the UK some people have started building old-fashioned dams using trees instead.

Caribbean
Hurricanes and storms cause massive loss of homes and lives in the USA and Caribbean. In the future, new homes that are designed to weather the storms using stronger materials will be more common.

Sweden

In Sweden they are experts at dealing with snow. Many houses have triple glazed windows to cope with cold weather. In the colder months, drivers switch to winter tyres.

They wear proper winter clothes too!

Sea levels around the world are rising. Cities like Venice, the Hague, Shanghai, Hong Kong, Miami, Rio de Janeiro and Osaka are at serious risk of flooding. High sea walls and other coastal defences help to stop flooding.

Those trees look cool.

China

Temperatures are higher in the city. To cope with the heat we need to plant more trees to provide shade and lower the air temperature.

The Netherlands

In the Netherlands 33 per cent of the land is below sea level and over 60 per cent of the land is at risk of flooding. The country has invested billions building dams, sea defences, canals and dikes to protect themselves.

Australia

Forest fires and bushfires are a big problem in the USA and Australia. One way to protect against fire is to start managed fires. Whole areas are cleared of vegetation which means the fire cannot spread.

Summer at Last!

It's summer again and the children are enjoying a walk together. In the past year they have learned so much about weather and climate. Sadly, they've also discovered more about climate change.

Weather is a wild and powerful thing. It feels impossible that the things we do can affect this mighty force of nature. But the children believe that each and everyone can do their bit to reduce the effects of climate change.

I'm angry – our future is in danger.

WILD WEATHER FACTS

Greta Thunberg is a schoolgirl from Sweden who has helped lots of people become more aware of climate change. She began campaigning outside parliament in Sweden. Now she leads a worldwide movement to combat climate change. Children all over the world are staging walkouts from school to put pressure on their governments to cut greenhouse gas emissions and promote green practices. Greta says 'time is running out' but there is hope if we take action now.

GET BUSY

You can help combat the effects of climate change with some quick and easy actions. Why not ask your parents if you can walk to school or to local shops instead of driving? Put on a jumper instead of turning the heating up. Ask local community leaders if you can plant some tree or a wildlife garden. There are lots of ways to make a difference.

Don't worry, it's not too late!

We can work together to fight climate change.

Climate change worries me all the time.

High on the hill the children look out to sea and watch the sunshine make the waves shimmer like gold. It's so beautiful that it's easy to forget that climate change is happening. We have a wonderful world but if we work together we can keep it that way.

45

Glossary

Air pressure When referring to weather this means the pressure of the Earth's atmosphere.

Atmosphere The gases that surround the Earth.

Carbon emissions The carbon dioxide that is produced from natural sources (respiration, decomposition and ocean release) and from human activity (deforestation, burning fossil fuels and industry).

Climate change The long-term changes in the Earth's weather patterns.

Concerto A musical piece written for a solo instrument, acocompanied by an orchestra.

Dikes High walls or dams that are built to stop flooding.

Equator The imaginary line around the circumference of the Earth that is halfway between the North and South Poles.

Extreme weather Weather that is very different to the usual or average pattern of weather. This could be something that happens over one day; like a flash flood or ice storm. It can also take place over time; like a heat wave.

Flood defences Anything that is done to prevent or control flooding. Methods can include planting vegetation, digging channels and canals or creating reservoirs and building walls, dams and barriers.

Greenhouse gases Gases in the Earth's atmosphere that trap radiation from the sun to create the 'greenhouse effect' and cause global warming.

Heat stroke Also called sunstroke, this is a health condition caused by exposure to too much heat. Expect high fever, headaches and even convulsions or coma.

Heatwave A long period of very hot weather.

Hexagonal Describes something with six sides. Hexagonal shapes in nature include snowflakes and cells of a honeycomb.

Humid Having a high amount of water vapour, which even on a hot day can make it feel damp, sticky or muggy.

Jet stream The band of strong, fast winds that circulates kilometres above the Earth's surface, often from west to east.

Long-term prediction/forecast Things that are expected to happen to the weather in the future. These predictions are made using information collected by scientific instruments at weather stations and from data gathered from weather satellites in space.

Meteorologist A scientist that studies the Earth's weather and atmosphere.

Monsoon A wind system of the Indian Ocean. In the summer it blows from the southwest and brings with it a season of heavy rain, referred to as Monsoon Rains.

Orbiting Moving in a circular path around another object. The solar system has planets (including Earth) and other objects which are orbiting around the sun.

Petrichor A pleasant earthy smell that rises up from dry soil during the first rain after a period of warm, dry weather.

Polar vortices At upper levels of the Earth's atmosphere at the North and South Pole there are wide areas of low pressure; each of which is called a polar vortex but together they form the polar vortices.

Sinkholes A hole formed in the ground when material underneath collapses. Sinkholes often appear after floods because soil or rocks are washed away.

Stratosphere The second major layer of the Earth's atmosphere which is found above the troposphere and below the mesosphere. Temperatures vary here with warmer temperatures up high and cooler temperatures nearer to Earth.

Troposphere The lowest level of the Earth's atmosphere and where most of the weather on Earth happens.

Water vapour Water in the form of gas.

Weather front When two different air masses meet they form a weather front. Each air masses has different temperatures and pressure so will create various kinds of weather.

 # Find out more

Friends of the Earth
https://friendsoftheearth.uk/climate-change

Friends of the Earth is a well established charity that tackles environmental matters. The organisation is international but promotes local solutions for the global crisis. You really can make your voice heard, petition, raise awareness and money in your local community to help our Earth.

Greenpeace
www.greenpeace.org.uk/challenges/climate-change

Get involved with protecting the planet and fighting climate change with Greenpeace. This organisation has campaigned to save the whale, protect the Amazon and look after our oceans for decades. Now they have joined the movement to fight climate change. Call to arrange a visit to your school from one of their many inspiring speakers.

NASA Climate Kids
https://climatekids.nasa.gov/how-to-help

Tackle climate change head on by making changes in your own life. This website suggests small things that you can do now and encourage the adults in your life to change too.

WWF
www.wwf.org.uk/get-involved/schools/resources/climate-change-resources

Knowledge is power and learning about climate change is important if we want to do something about it. One of the most respected charities for wildlife has compiled resources for teachers and children to use in their classrooms.

Index